Y0-AGK-254

IT'S HARD TO HUG A COW

written by
Su Colstrom

illustrated by
Susie Wecker

Rowe Publishing

Text copyright © 2016 by Su Colstrom
Illustration copyright © 2016 by Susie Wecker
All rights reserved.

ISBN 13: 978-1-939054-62-3
ISBN 10: 1-939054-62-1

No portion of this work may be used or reproduced in any manner whatsoever without written permission, except in the case of brief quotations embodied in articles and reviews.

1 3 5 7 9 8 6 4 2

Printed in the United States of America
Published by

R
Rowe Publishing

www.rowepub.com
Stockton, Kansas

DEDICATED TO...

I want to express my heart felt gratitude to my best friend and husband, Bill, as well as my friends and family for supporting my cow addiction. Also, in loving memory of two beautiful souls who shared their knowledge and love of cattle, Ben and Nadine Winans.

—Su Colstrom

For my beautiful daughters, Alex, Bette, and Eva, who inspire me to create with passion, love with my whole heart, and speak truth through my work.

For Chris, Mom and Dad, and my family and dear friends, for your love and encouragement.

Last, but not least, for Pam Foster; the wonderful teacher who first introduced me to writing and illustration during middle school.

—Susie Wecker

About This Book

This book is about my cow named Chloe. She is a Registered Red Angus.

Chloe was born in 2007, and she has had three sets of twins. Twin births are rare; occurring in only seven percent or less of births depending on breed and genetics. Having three sets of twins makes Chloe extra special!

BUT

should you,

could you,

just how

would you

hug a cow?

Well, the head on approach just might work, or **NOT**.

Perhaps the opposite end approach, moo-st definitely **NOT!**

You could try
a great big
bear hug to the
tummy, but hold
on, on, on!!!!!!

Watch **out-ch**
for the cactus!

Hopping on
Chloe's back
might work, **whoa**
what a bumpy ride!

OH! OH! OH!

I know **now**

just **how**

to hug

this

cow!

How about a loving, **tender hug** around the side of Chloe's neck?

That works great, but watch your **toes**!

Fun Cow Facts

- The first cows in the Americas arrived with Christopher Columbus on his second voyage.
- Cows are red-green colorblind.
- The average cow chews at least 50 times per minute.
- Cows drink the equivalent of a bathtub full of water each day.
- Cows actually do not bite grass; instead they curl their tongue around it.
- Cows have almost total 360-degree panoramic vision, with blind spots only right in front of and behind them.
- Cows have a single stomach, but four different digestive compartments.
- Cows are pregnant for 9 months just like people.
- Cows spend 8 hours per day eating, 8 hours chewing their cud (regurgitated, partially digested food), and 8 hours sleeping.
- You can lead a cow upstairs, but not downstairs. Cows knees can't bend properly to walk downstairs.
- Cows can't vomit.
- The average cow produces 70 lbs. of milk. That's 8 gallons per day!
- Cows only have teeth on the bottom.
- Cows have a great sense of smell. They can smell something up to 6 miles away.
- The average cow will eat about 100 lbs. of feed per day.
- When cows digest food, fermentation results; cattle produce 250 to 500 liters of the gas per day.
- There are about 350 udder squirts in a gallon of milk.
- Researchers have found that if you name a cow and treat her as an individual, she will produce almost 500 more pints of milk a year.
- These extremely social creatures don't like to be alone. So if a cow isolates herself, she's either not feeling well or she's about to give birth.
- A cow produces between 40 and 150 liters (10–45 gallons) of saliva per day, depending on the feed she receives.
- Red Angus Cattle are more heat tolerant than black. The majority of the world's cattle are in areas that need heat tolerance, so the red color is a definite advantage.

Sources:
- The Dairy Guy. (2012). *Interesting Facts about Cows.* Dairy Moos. www.dairymoos.com
- Red Angus Association of America. www.redangus.org

CPSIA information can be obtained
at www.ICGtesting.com
Printed in the USA
LVOW05*0832210516

489359LV00003B/4/P

9 781939 054623